PRAYING A SCRIPTURAL ROSARY

Fr Guy Nicholls

All booklets are published thanks to the generosity of the supporters of the Catholic Truth Society

ISBN 978 1 78469 734 1

Contents

What is a Scriptural Rosary and how is it prayed?

The Rosary is Christ-centred Meditation and Prayer

Although the Rosary is closely associated with our Lady, and justly so, it is principally a systematic meditation on the Incarnation and work of her Son, our Lord Jesus Christ. In the Rosary, we contemplate Emmanuel, God-with-us, as he was born of the Virgin Mary, as he ministered in Galilee and Judaea, as he suffered and died in Jerusalem and as he was raised to new life and to heavenly glory which he shares with us first through the outpouring of the Holy Spirit and also by the promise and foretaste of eternal life with him in heaven, which our Lady already fully shares there with him.

These meditations are inspired by twenty distinct episodes, the 'mysteries of the Rosary' as they are called, on each of which we reflect in turn, doing so in the company of the Blessed Mother of God. So complete is the range of the mysteries in which we ponder the journey of Christ's life, death and resurrection in the Rosary that Pope St Paul VI, borrowing a phrase from Pope Pius XII, described it as a 'compendium of the entire Gospel'.[1] So central is the role which we invite our Lady to exercise with us on this journey that Pope St John Paul II summed up the entire Rosary as contemplating the Face of Christ with Mary.

But what do we mean by the word 'mysteries' with reference to the prayer of the Rosary? In the Christian tradition, the word 'mystery' refers to God's grace which, though hidden from our senses, is nonetheless powerfully alive and active in us spiritually. 'Mystery' has a related meaning in connection with the Faith, referring to particular truths which God has revealed, and which surpass our powers of full comprehension, such as the Blessed Trinity, the Incarnation of the Son of God as man, or the real presence of Christ in the Blessed Sacrament under the outward appearances of bread and wine. Yet although we cannot fully grasp such realities because they far surpass our power to understand them completely, we are nonetheless given the grace and power to understand them sufficiently to be able to enter into their inner reality beyond our natural power of comprehension. In this way God grants us an insight into his loving way of dealing with us by drawing us into an ever greater and more fruitful union with himself. 'Mystery' as we use the word in the Rosary describes an event into which we enter spiritually by pondering it and using it to enrich our prayer so as to bring us into

1 Pope Paul VI, *Marialis Cultus*, Apostolic Exhortation on devotion to our Lady, Rome, 1974, para. 42

closer union with Christ the Son of God and Redeemer of the entire human race.

The historic or classic arrangement of the Mysteries divides them into three main groups, the Joyful, Sorrowful and the Glorious which focus in turn on five 'moments' or scenes in the earliest years of Christ's life, five more in his Passion and Death, and five in his triumphant Resurrection and its consequences for us. To these Pope St John Paul II added the optional five Mysteries of Light, to fill in a gap between the Joyful and the Sorrowful mysteries, through the commemoration of five special 'luminous' events or aspects of our Lord's earthly ministry, from his Baptism to the Last Supper, which shed light upon his work of salvation.

Meditating upon the Word of God

These mysteries on which we meditate, then, are drawn principally from the Gospel accounts of the Incarnation, the Public Ministry, the Passion and Death, and the Resurrection and Glorification of the Son of God made man. We contemplate each of them in turn by placing ourselves into the company of his Blessed Mother. Pope St John Paul II, in his 2003 Apostolic Letter *Rosarium Virginis Mariae* (*The Rosary of the Virgin Mary*), beautifully described the praying of the Rosary as "nothing other than to contemplate with Mary the face of Christ".[2] For as we greet her in the constant repetition

---

2 Pope John Paul II, *Rosarium Virginis Mariae*, Apostolic Letter on the Most Holy Rosary, Rome, 2002, para. 3 (RVM)

of the prayer we call the 'Ave Maria' or 'Hail Mary', we follow our Lady's example as laid down in the Scriptures: *"Mary treasured all these things and pondered them in her heart"* (*Lk* 2:19,51). The 'Hail Mary' is itself a prayer inspired by the two scriptural greetings to our Lady before our Lord's birth, those of Gabriel (*Lk* 1:28) and Elizabeth (*Lk* 1:42). As we continually repeat this prayer, we call upon our Lady to guide us and to show herself to us as the model for our prayer. In this way together with her we ponder or contemplate the mysteries of our redemption, a redemption which she shares with us and which she has already reached its fulness in her glorious Assumption and Crowning in Heaven.

As the first of all the redeemed, she is both our companion in meditation and our guide, for under the direction of the Holy Spirit she constantly deepened her union with her Divine Son. We recall in Scripture that when a woman in the crowd, lost in admiration for our Lord, raised her voice loudly in his mother's praise, *"Blessed is the womb that bore you, and the breasts at which you nursed"*, he pointed out in reply that *"Blessed rather are those who hear the word of God and keep it"* (*Lk* 11:27, 28). When we reflect on these words, we remember that our Lord's Mother was certainly the greatest practitioner of 'hearing and keeping the word of God'. As St Augustine said, *"Mary conceived the Word in her heart before she conceived him in her body"*.[3] From

[3] St Augustine, *De Sancta Virginitate*, PL 40, 398

the time of the Annunciation onwards she continually lived the mysteries of her Son, not only in the sense that she was a personal witness to most of them, but in the deeper sense that she put into practice all that is contained in them. She, more than anyone, can be said to have 'imitated what they contain', and thereby 'obtained what they promise'.

So, in meditating on these mysteries of the Life, Death and Resurrection of God's only-begotten Son, we are the more empowered to enter into their inner strength by keeping company with our Lady, by constantly invoking her as we call upon her by name. There is a prayer attributed to Cardinal Wiseman in which we find the words: "*May her sweet name be lisped by little ones, and linger on the lips of the aged and the dying*". At the beginning of the first part of each 'Hail Mary' we call upon her by name, the woman who is full of God's grace, and at the beginning of the second part we repeat her name: "Holy Mary, Mother of God, pray for us sinners", meaning that during the course of our praying any one mystery we will have called on her by name twenty times to pray with us and for us.

The Rosary is for everyone

The Rosary is a prayer suited to persons of all ages and conditions, young or old, sophisticated or simple. It is suitable to be said alone or with others, slowly and interwoven with sentences of Scripture or frequent pauses, or rhythmically like a march. It is suited to be prayed when we ourselves are joyful or sorrowful, for ourselves or for others in whatever need, and in union with the whole Church praying to Christ her Son.

Let us look at the four great cycles of the Rosary mysteries: Joy, Light, Sorrow and Glory. How do these sum up our faith, and what can we gain from them?

We can take note, first of all, that our Lord is at the heart of every mystery, and as we consider each in turn we will see just how that is so. But we will also find out by praying each of these mysteries in company with our Lord's Mother, just how she is present to us and how she points us towards him, how she teaches us to see him as though with her own eyes of perfect faith, hope and love.

In the Joyful Mysteries we enter with Mary into five events "marked by the joy radiating from the event of the Incarnation".[4] In all five of these events Scripture shows us the vitally important part that our Lady plays in bringing about her Son's presence in the world and in his growth towards human maturity.

In the Mysteries of Light we come into the presence of Christ in his public ministry, the 'light of the world' (*Jn* 8:12) who proclaims the Gospel of God's Kingdom which is now present in the world in himself, above all as he manifests his glory in the Transfiguration and as he gives us his Body and Blood in the Eucharist. In these events, although Scripture does not tell us that our Lady was present in all as she was in the joyful

---

4 RVM, 20

mysteries, nonetheless her presence at the wedding in Cana, and her providential role there in bringing about her Son's first great sign, becomes an important indication to us of the importance of her quiet and undemonstrative presence in the background of her Son's ministry and her role in mediating between her Son and all who need his divine intervention, who need to be taught how to ask for it.

In the Sorrowful Mysteries, Scripture tells us of Mary's presence in the culminating event of them all: the crucifixion and death of her Son, in which she shares in a singular way in the work which he here accomplishes. Here at Calvary where she received us as her children at the foot of her Son's Cross, and so took upon herself the care of us as her own children, she continually helps us to understand what it means for each one of us to take up our cross daily and follow Christ.

Finally, in the Glorious Mysteries, our Lady's presence is explicitly witnessed by Scripture in the event of the Descent of the Holy Spirit at Pentecost, but Scripture also shows in a hidden way her presence in glory at the end of her life on earth, when her Son brings her to share fully in his triumphal and glorious entry to heaven, just as she had shared faithfully in his suffering and Cross.

The Prayers of the Rosary

Each mystery begins with the prayer we know as the 'Lord's Prayer', or, from its opening words, as the 'Our

Father'. It is fitting that we begin our contemplation of each aspect of our Lord's saving work using our Lord's own words in which he taught his disciples to pray to 'our Father in heaven'. Our Lord is recorded in the Gospels as praying to his Father, 'Abba, Father,' (e.g. *Mk* 14:36) and he invites us also to turn with him to God as *our* Father in this wonderful prayer which sums up all praise and petition we can ever make.

The 'Hail Mary' is the most substantial element in the Rosary and because it is addressed to our Lady, it is the one which makes the Rosary a Marian Prayer *par excellence*. Yet at the same time it is at its heart a Christ-centred prayer, literally, since the central word of the prayer is the announcement of the holy name of the fruit of Mary's womb, Jesus her Son. The prayer begins with two quotations from Scripture, in which the Virgin Mary is greeted first by God's own heavenly messenger, Gabriel, who announces her as the woman 'full of grace', (*Lk* 1:28) and then the ecstatic words of her kinswoman Elizabeth at her visitation, "blessed are you among women and blessed is the fruit of your womb!"(*Lk* 1:42) This double greeting establishes for us Mary's status both in God's eyes, and in ours: she is the fully-graced Mother of our Redeemer. We, too, echo these greetings whenever we say this prayer, calling upon our Lady to lend her aid to us as we enter into contemplation of each of the mysteries of our Redemption. The prayer comes to a central climax in the naming of Jesus, and thereafter we continue our prayer to our heavenly

Mother, begging her to intercede for us 'now and at the hour of our death.' Thus the ten repetitions of the 'Hail Mary' in each mystery find their high point in the ten repetitions of the name of her divine Son. She is the God-bearer, the *Theotokos*, whom we are inviting to draw us into her contemplation as she gazes on her Son, seen in the Gospel events by which he has redeemed us.

Finally, the 'Glory be to the Father' is the doxology, that is the prayer of praise and thanksgiving in which we give glory to the Trinity: Father, Son and Holy Spirit by whom we have been created, by whose love we have been redeemed and for whose glory we are called to live with him for all eternity, 'world without end'. For just as the Eucharistic Prayer at the heart of the Mass culminates in a doxology of praise to the Blessed Trinity, "through him (Christ) and with him and in him, O God almighty Father, in the unity of the Holy Spirit, all glory and honour is yours, for ever and ever", so too does each mystery of the Rosary end in praise of the Blessed Trinity, thus showing that, far from being in conflict with the Liturgy, the Rosary demonstrates a kinship with the sacrifice of the Mass itself.

The Scriptures and the Rosary

The Scriptures are a window to enlighten our understanding of Christ. The ancient practice of a slow and prayerful reading of Scripture, known as *lectio divina* (literally 'divine reading') is very easily combined with the praying of the Rosary, so that both can benefit the one who uses them together. In the company of Mary and being taught by her we can further deepen our contemplation in this school of the 'art of prayer'.[5]

How to combine the Rosary with Sacred Scripture

We can pray the Rosary on our own or with others. In both cases we can use the Scriptures to enhance our entry into the heart of the mystery.

It is good to begin by praying the Lord's Prayer, the Hail Mary three times and the Creed in order to settle ourselves into the company of our Lady, as it were, and to place ourselves under her guidance and protection as we also renew the profession of our faith.

A group of mysteries is announced, depending on your own choice, or according to the custom of selecting a group associated with the different days of the week. For instance, it is customary to pray the Glorious Mysteries on the Lord's day, Sunday, the day of the Resurrection, and also on Wednesday; since the Joyful Mysteries are especially connected with our Lady's part in her Son's coming into this world, they are prayed on Saturday, the weekday associated particularly with her in the liturgy, and also on Monday; the Sorrowful Mysteries, which are entirely focused on our Lord's Passion are therefore especially prayed on Friday, the day of our Lord's suffering and crucifixion, and also on Tuesday; and the Mysteries of Light, which culminate

---

5 RVM, 5

in the Institution of the Blessed Eucharist, are prayed particularly on Thursday, since that is the day on which our Lord celebrated the Last Supper with his Apostles, the event which is contemplated in the fifth Mystery of Light.

Each mystery may be introduced by a short title which describes exactly what is to be contemplated in it.

After this the first passage of Scripture is read, which sums up the central meaning of the mystery as a whole, announced to us in God's own words. Then the Our Father is prayed in the usual way; either directly all through by one person alone, or in two parts, where one person prays the first part and the rest take up the second part of the prayer from 'Give us this day our daily bread' to the end. Following that, each 'Hail Mary' is introduced by its own short scriptural sentence. Generally these sentences form a sequence punctuated by the prayers, helping to unfold the mystery progressively. Quite frequently these sentences may be part of a single passage divided so that we can savour it while reciting the 'Hail Mary', before moving on to the next. Occasionally the sentences may be drawn from different passages or even from different books, so as to illustrate how the Old Testament and the New are complementary. The final sentence, which leads into the concluding doxology, the 'Glory be to the Father', acts as a summary or closure to the mystery before we move to the next one.

Concluding prayers

Having finished the mystery or mysteries we have chosen to pray, it is customary to conclude with the 'Salve Regina', known in its familiar translation as "Hail, holy Queen, Mother of mercy." This wonderful prayer from the late Middle Ages has for many generations of Christians expressed our love for our gentle yet powerful Mother and our crying out to her for aid in all our many needs, sorrows and difficulties in this life of exile from our true heavenly homeland, until that day when, together with her, we will at last behold her Son face to face in glory.

Finally, in the Collect prayer we sum up and gather together all the intentions for which we have offered our prayers. We call to mind that God's only-begotten Son has brought about our redemption by his life, death and resurrection, the events of which we have contemplated in the joyful and luminous, the sorrowful and glorious mysteries respectively. The prayer describes this work of our redemption as a 'purchase', meaning that our Lord has procured or ransomed us by freely giving his life up for us, not as a financial transaction but as a sacrifice of love. In the end, however, his suffering and death have been transformed into the glory of his Resurrection and Ascension by means of which he also transforms us through the outpouring of his Holy Spirit.

Out of this reflection on our redemption which has already been won for us, we pray that by meditating on these mysteries, "we may both imitate what they contain and obtain what they promise." This is a request for two special graces; first, that we may come more and more to resemble our Lord and his Mother in their love and humility, in their sacred humanity and submission to the will of the Father, and secondly that we may both understand what we have prayed about and through that deepening of our understanding we may be made ready to share in the heavenly realities that they have opened the way for us to enter into. For the end of all our praying is that we should come at last to our heavenly home and see our Lady and our Lord face to face for all eternity in the joy which surpasses all our powers of imagination.

Using this book to pray

We pray that in contemplating the mysteries of the Rosary, "we may both imitate what they contain and obtain what they promise". Each set of mysteries is preceded by short meditations to help us consider what those two petitions mean as we pray each set of mysteries, as well as each individual mystery. Following these are passages from Scripture to use when praying a Scriptural Rosary, meditating on each passage in turn whilst praying the *Our Father*, *Hail Mary*, or *Glory be* with the prayers clearly marked so that you can simply follow consecutively from the beginning of the mystery to the end.

The Joyful Mysteries of the Rosary

The five Joyful Mysteries are all scenes of the earliest years of our Lord's earthly life, from the announcement of his Advent or Coming, to his own declaration of his divine Sonship in the Temple at Jerusalem when he was about twelve years old. In all of them our Lady plays an especially significant role. We ask her to let us accompany her as we meditate on them.

FIRST JOYFUL MYSTERY

The Annunciation by the Angel Gabriel to Our Lady

The Annunciation teaches us our Lady's total submission to God's will. Her heart was already turned perfectly towards God when Gabriel was sent to invite her to be the Mother of the only-begotten Son of God. We pray that our Lady may show us that we can be confident in leaving all to God's providence, just as she always did.

Again the Lord spoke to Ahaz: "Ask a sign of the Lord your God; let it be as deep as Sheol or as high as heaven". But Ahaz said, "I will not ask, and I will not put the Lord to the test." And he said, "Hear then, O house of David! Is it too little for you to weary men, that you weary my God also? Therefore the Lord himself will give you a sign. Behold, the virgin shall conceive and bear a son, and shall call his name Immanuel." (*Is* 7:10-14)

Our Father...

In the sixth month the angel Gabriel was sent from God to a city of Galilee named Nazareth, to a virgin betrothed to a man whose name was Joseph, of the house of David. And the virgin's name was Mary. (*Lk* 1:26-27)

Hail Mary...

And he came to her and said, "Greetings, O highly favoured one, the Lord is with you!" (*Lk* 1:28)

Hail Mary...

But she was greatly troubled at the saying, and tried to discern what sort of greeting this might be. (*Lk* 1:29)

Hail Mary...

And the angel said to her, "Do not be afraid, Mary; for you have won favour with God." (*Lk* 1:30)

Hail Mary...

"And behold, you will conceive in your womb and bear a son, and you shall call his name Jesus." (*Lk* 1:31)

Hail Mary...

“He will be great and will be called the Son of the Most High.” (*Lk* 1:32a)

Hail Mary...

“And the Lord God will give to him the throne of his father David, and he will reign over the house of Jacob for ever, and of his kingdom there will be no end.” (*Lk* 1:32b-33)

Hail Mary...

And Mary said to the angel, “How will this be, since I am a virgin?” (*Lk* 1:34)

Hail Mary...

And the angel answered her, “The Holy Spirit will come upon you, and the power of the Most High will overshadow you; therefore the child to be born will be called holy – the Son of God.” (*Lk* 1:35)

Hail Mary...

“And behold, your relative Elizabeth in her old age has also conceived a son, and this is the sixth month with her who was called barren. For nothing is impossible with God”. (*Lk* 1:36-7)

Hail Mary...

And Mary said, “Behold, I am the servant of the Lord; let it be to me according to your word.” And the angel departed from her. (*Lk* 1:38)

Glory be to the Father...

SECOND JOYFUL MYSTERY

The Visitation by Our Lady to her Kinswoman Elizabeth

The Visitation shows us a perfect example of our Lady's unselfishness. Having heard the Angel's message concerning her kinswoman, Elizabeth, Mary is anxious to be of assistance to her in whatever way she can. In her canticle, the 'Magnificat' we pray to share in the joy and greater love of God that Mary's unselfish love for others brings.

Sing aloud, O daughter of Zion; shout, O Israel! Rejoice and exult with all your heart, O daughter of Jerusalem! The Lord has taken away the judgements against you; he has cleared away your enemies. The king of Israel, the Lord, is in your midst; you shall never again fear evil. (*Zp* 3:14-15)

Our Father...

In those days Mary arose and went with haste into the hill country, to a town in Judah, and she entered the house of Zechariah and greeted Elizabeth. (*Lk* 1:39-40)

Hail Mary...

And when Elizabeth heard the greeting of Mary, the baby leaped in her womb. And Elizabeth was filled with the Holy Spirit. (*Lk* 1:41)

Hail Mary...

And she exclaimed with a loud cry, "Blessed are you among women, and blessed is the fruit of your womb! And why is this granted to me, that the mother of my Lord should come to me?" (*Lk* 1:42-43)

Hail Mary...

"For behold, when the sound of your greeting came to my ears, the baby in my womb leaped for joy." (*Lk* 1:44)

Hail Mary...

"And blessed is she who believed that there would be a fulfilment of what was spoken to her from the Lord." (*Lk* 1:45)

Hail Mary...

And Mary said, “My soul magnifies the Lord and my spirit rejoices in God my Saviour, for he has looked on the humble estate of his servant.” (*Lk* 1:46-48a)

Hail Mary...

“For behold, from now on all generations will call me blessed; for he who is mighty has done great things for me.” (*Lk* 1:48b-49a)

Hail Mary...

“Holy is his name. And his mercy is for those who fear him from generation to generation.” (*Lk* 1:49b-50)

Hail Mary...

“He has shown strength with his arm; he has scattered the proud in the thoughts of their hearts; he has brought down the mighty from their thrones and exalted those of humble estate; he has filled the hungry with good things, and the rich he has sent away empty.” (*Lk* 1:51-53)

Hail Mary...

“He has helped his servant Israel, in remembrance of his mercy, as he spoke to our fathers, to Abraham and to his offspring for ever.” (*Lk* 1:54-55)

Hail Mary...

And Mary remained with her about three months and returned to her home. (*Lk* 1:56)

Glory be to the Father...

THIRD JOYFUL MYSTERY

The Birth of Our Saviour at Bethlehem in Judæa

The Nativity shows us the humility of Mary and Jesus, in that they do not spurn poverty when he enters this world as our Saviour and King, and as lowly Mary's Son. We share in this mystery the wonder with which the young mother gazed with adoration upon her divine Son's face. We pray for the humility that sets us free from fear of the respect of others.

For to us a child is born, to us a son is given; and the government shall be upon his shoulder, and his name shall be called Wonderful Counsellor, Mighty God, Everlasting Father, Prince of Peace. (*Is* 9:5)

Our Father...

In those days a decree went out from Caesar Augustus that all the world should be registered. This was the first registration when Quirinius was governor of Syria. And all went to be registered, each to his own town. (*Lk* 2:1-3)

Hail Mary...

And Joseph also went up from Galilee, from the town of Nazareth, to Judaea, to the city of David, which is called Bethlehem, because he was of the house and lineage of David, to be registered with Mary, his betrothed, who was with child. (*Lk* 2:4-5)

Hail Mary...

And while they were there, the time came for her to give birth. And she gave birth to her firstborn son. (*Lk* 2:6-7a)

Hail Mary...

She wrapped him in swaddling cloths, and laid him in a manger, because there was no place for them in the inn. (*Lk* 2:7b)

Hail Mary...

And in the same region there were shepherds out in the field, keeping watch over their flock by night. And an angel of the Lord appeared to them, and the glory of the Lord shone around them. (*Lk* 2:8-9a)

5 *Hail Mary...*

And they were filled with great fear. And the angel said to them "Fear not, for behold, I bring you good news of great joy that will be for all the people. For unto you is born this day in the city of David a Saviour, who is Christ the Lord." (*Lk* 2:9b-11)

6 *Hail Mary...*

"And this will be a sign for you: you will find a baby wrapped in swaddling cloths and lying in a manger." (*Lk* 2:12)

7 *Hail Mary...*

And suddenly there was with the angel a multitude of the heavenly host praising God and saying, "Glory to God in the highest, and on earth peace among those with whom he is pleased." (*Lk* 2:13-14)

8 *Hail Mary...*

When the angels went away from them into heaven, the shepherds said to one another, "Let us go over to Bethlehem and see this thing that has happened, which the Lord has made known to us." (*Lk* 2:15)

9 *Hail Mary...*

And they went with haste and found Mary and Joseph, and the baby lying in the manger. And when they saw it, they made known the saying that had been told them concerning this child. And all who heard it wondered at what the shepherds told them. (*Lk* 2:16-18)

Hail Mary...

But Mary treasured up all these things, pondering them in her heart. And the shepherds returned, glorifying and praising God for all they had heard and seen, as it had been told them. (*Lk* 2:19-20)

Glory be to the Father...

FOURTH JOYFUL MYSTERY

The Presentation of Our Lord in the Temple

The Presentation in the Temple exemplifies our Lady's purity and obedience to God's Law. We contemplate the joy and gratitude with which she brings her Son to the Temple, and contemplate with her the prophecy of Simeon foretelling the suffering of her heart in union with her Son's redemptive suffering in his passion. We pray for the grace to accept God's plan for us whatever it may involve.

"Behold, I send my messenger, and he will prepare the way before me. And the Lord whom you seek will suddenly come to his temple; and the messenger of the covenant in whom you delight, behold, he is coming, says the Lord of hosts." (*Ml* 3:1)

Our Father...

And when the time came for their purification according to the Law of Moses, they brought him to Jerusalem to present him to the Lord (as it is written in the Law of the Lord, "Every male who first opens the womb shall be called holy to the Lord") and to offer a sacrifice according to what is said in the Law of the Lord, "a pair of turtle-doves, or two young pigeons". (*Lk* 2:22-24)

Hail Mary...

Now there was a man in Jerusalem, whose name was Simeon, and this man was righteous and devout, waiting for the consolation of Israel, and the Holy Spirit was upon him. (*Lk* 2:25)

Hail Mary...

And it had been revealed to him by the Holy Spirit that he would not see death before he had seen the Lord's Christ. (*Lk* 2:26)

Hail Mary...

And he came in the Spirit into the temple, and when the parents brought in the child Jesus, to do for him according to the custom of the Law, he took him up in his arms and blessed God. (*Lk* 2:27-28)

Hail Mary...

And Simeon said, "Lord, now you are letting your servant depart in peace, as according to your word; for my eyes have seen your salvation that you have prepared in the presence of all peoples, a light for revelation to the Gentiles, and for glory to your people Israel." (*Lk* 2:29-32)

Hail Mary...

And his father and his mother marvelled at what was said about him. And Simeon blessed them and said to Mary his mother, "Behold, this child is appointed for the fall and rising of many in Israel, and for a sign that is opposed." (*Lk* 2:33-34)

Hail Mary...

"And a sword will pierce through your own soul also, so that the thoughts from many hearts may be revealed." (*Lk* 2:35)

Hail Mary...

And there was a prophetess, Anna, the daughter of Phanuel, of the tribe of Asher. She was advanced in years, having lived with her husband seven years from when she was a virgin, and then as a widow until she was eighty-four. She did not depart from the temple, worshipping with fasting and prayer night and day. (*Lk* 2:36-37)

Hail Mary...

And coming up at that very hour she began to give thanks to God and to speak of him to all who were waiting for the redemption of Jerusalem. (*Lk* 2:38)
Hail Mary...

And when they had performed everything according to the Law of the Lord, they returned into Galilee, to their own town of Nazareth. (*Lk* 2:39)
Hail Mary...

And the child grew and became strong, filled with wisdom. And the favour of God was upon him. (*Lk* 2:40)
Glory be to the Father...

FIFTH JOYFUL MYSTERY

Our Lord is Found Among the Doctors in the Temple

The Finding of the Child Jesus in the Temple shows us our Lady's patience in adversity and our Lord's own understanding of his divinity. From this mystery we learn to wait for God to reveal his will to us in his own time, trusting that he knows what is best for us. We ask her to help us to do what she learned from this event, to trust God's good will towards his children.

For the Lord honoured the father above the children, and he confirmed the judgement of the mother over her sons. Whoever honours his father atones for sins, and whoever glorifies his mother is like one who lays up treasure. (*Si* 3:2-4)
Our Father...

Now his parents went to Jerusalem every year at the Feast of the Passover. (*Lk* 2:41)
Hail Mary...

And when he was twelve years old, they went up according to custom. (*Lk* 2:42)
Hail Mary...

And when the feast was ended, as they were returning, the boy Jesus stayed behind in Jerusalem. His parents did not know it. (*Lk* 2:43)
Hail Mary...

But supposing him to be in the group they went a day's journey, but then they began to search for him among their relatives and acquaintances. (*Lk* 2:44)
Hail Mary...

And when they did not find him, they returned to Jerusalem, searching for him. (*Lk* 2:45)
Hail Mary...

After three days they found him in the temple, sitting among the teachers, listening to them and asking them questions. (*Lk* 2:46)

Hail Mary...

And all who heard him were amazed at his understanding and his answers. (*Lk* 2:47)

Hail Mary...

And when his parents saw him, they were astonished. And his mother said to him, "Son, why have you treated us so? Behold, your father and I have been searching for you in great distress." (*Lk* 2:48)

Hail Mary...

And he said to them, "Why were you looking for me? Did you not know that I must be in my Father's house?" And they did not understand the saying that he spoke to them. (*Lk* 2:49-50)

Hail Mary...

And he went down with them and came to Nazareth and was submissive to them. (*Lk* 2:51a)

Hail Mary...

And his mother treasured up all these things in her heart. And Jesus increased in wisdom and in stature and in favour with God and man. (*Lk* 2:51b-52)

Glory be to the Father...

The Luminous Mysteries of the Rosary

The five Mysteries of Light illustrate various features of the ministry of Christ which is itself a continual revelation of Christ as the 'light of the world' (Jn *8:12*). *In them we see our Lord as the incarnate revelation of God's Kingdom, transforming the darkness of the world by the light of his teaching, his miracles and his consoling presence.*

FIRST LUMINOUS MYSTERY

The Baptism of Our Lord by John in the River Jordan

In the Baptism of our Lord we meditate on the innocent one who 'became sin' for our sake by descending into the waters; we behold the manifestation of the Holy Trinity in the Father's voice and Spirit's anointing of the Son for his ministry. We pray that the grace of our own anointing in baptism may be fruitful in our lives.

In those days Jesus came from Nazareth of Galilee and was baptised by John in the Jordan. (*Mk* 1:9)
Our Father...

John saw Jesus coming toward him, and said, "Behold, the Lamb of God, who takes away the sin of the world!" (*Jn* 1:29)
Hail Mary...

John would have prevented him, saying, "I need to be baptised by you, and do you come to me?" (*Mt* 3:14)
Hail Mary...

But Jesus answered him, "Let it be so now; for thus it is fitting for us to fulfil all righteousness." Then John consented. (*Mt* 3:15)
Hail Mary...

And when Jesus was baptised, immediately he went up from the water, and behold, the heavens were opened to him, and he saw the Spirit of God descending like a dove, and coming to rest on him. (*Mt* 3:16)
Hail Mary...

And a voice came from heaven, "You are my beloved Son; with you I am well pleased." (*Mk* 1:11)
Hail Mary...

John the Baptist preached, saying, "After me comes he who is mightier than I, the strap of whose sandals I am not worthy to stoop down and untie." (*Mk* 1:7)
Hail Mary...

"I have baptised you with water; but he will baptise you with the Holy Spirit." (*Mk* 1:8)
Hail Mary...

"I myself did not know him; but he who sent me to baptise with water said to me, 'He on whom you see the Spirit descend and remain, this is he who baptises with the Holy Spirit.'" (*Jn* 1:33)
Hail Mary...

"This is he of whom I said, 'After me comes a man who ranks before me, for he was before me.'" (*Jn* 1:30)
Hail Mary...

And John bore witness, "I saw the Spirit descend as a dove from heaven, and it remained on him." (*Jn* 1:32)
Hail Mary...

"And I have seen and have borne witness that this is the Son of God." (*Jn* 1:34)
Glory be to the Father...

SECOND LUMINOUS MYSTERY

Our Lord's First Miracle at the Wedding Feast at Cana

At Cana we contemplate how our Lady perceived her Son's compassion and anticipated his will to save those in distress. Thanks to the intercession of his mother, the first among believers, our Lord changes water into wine and opens the hearts of his disciples to faith. We pray that our faith may be strengthened and find joy through the new wine of the Sacraments.

There was a wedding at Cana in Galilee, and the mother of Jesus was there. (*Jn* 2:1)

Our Father…

Jesus also was invited to the wedding with his disciples. (*Jn* 2:2)

Hail Mary…

When the wine ran out, the mother of Jesus said to him, "They have no wine." (*Jn* 2:3)

Hail Mary…

And Jesus said to her, "Woman, what does this have to do with me? My hour has not yet come." (*Jn* 2:4)

Hail Mary…

His mother said to the servants, "Do whatever he tells you." (*Jn* 2:5)

Hail Mary…

Now there were six stone jars there for the Jewish rites of purification, each holding twenty or thirty gallons. (*Jn* 2:6)

Hail Mary…

Jesus said to the servants, "Fill the jars with water." And they filled them up to the brim. (*Jn* 2:7)

Hail Mary…

And he said to them, "Now draw some out, and take it to the master of the feast." So they took it. (*Jn* 2:8)

Hail Mary…

When the master of the feast tasted the water, it had become wine. (*Jn* 2:9a)

Hail Mary…

He did not know where it came from (though the servants who had drawn the water knew). (*Jn* 2:9b)

Hail Mary…

The master of the feast called the bridegroom and said to him, "Everyone serves the good wine first, and when people have drunk freely, then the poor wine. But you have kept the good wine until now." (*Jn* 2:9b-10)

Hail Mary…

This, the first of his signs, Jesus did at Cana in Galilee, and manifested his glory. And his disciples believed in him. (*Jn* 2:11)

Glory be to the Father...

THIRD LUMINOUS MYSTERY

The Preaching of the Kingdom

Jesus proclaims the coming of the Kingdom of God and calls to conversion all who hear him in humble trust. We rejoice to contemplate the inauguration of that ministry of mercy on earth which he continues to exercise until the end of time and we pray that we may be given the grace of true conversion and final perseverance in faith.

The land of Zebulun and the land of Naphtali, the way of the sea, beyond the Jordan, Galilee of the Gentiles - the people dwelling in darkness have seen a great light, and for those dwelling in the region and shadow of death, on them a light has dawned. (*Mt* 4:15-16; quoting *Is* 9:2)

Our Father...

And leaving Nazareth Jesus went and dwelt in Capernaum by the sea, in the territory of Zebulun and Naphtali, that what was spoken by the prophet Isaiah might be fulfilled. (*Mt* 4:13-14)

Hail Mary...

Jesus came into Galilee, proclaiming the gospel of God, and saying, "The time is fulfilled, and the kingdom of God is at hand; repent and believe in the gospel." (*Mk* 1:15)

Hail Mary...

And Jesus returned in the power of the Spirit into Galilee, and a report about him went out through all the surrounding country. And he taught in their synagogues, being glorified by all. (*Lk* 4:14-15)

Hail Mary...

And he came to Nazareth, where he had been brought up. And as was his custom, he went to the synagogue on the Sabbath day, and he stood up to read. And the scroll of the prophet Isaiah was given to him. (*Lk* 4:16-17a)

Hail Mary...

He unrolled the scroll and found the place where it was written, "The Spirit of the Lord is upon me, because he has anointed me to proclaim good news to the poor." (*Lk* 4:17b-18a)

5 *Hail Mary...*

"He has sent me to proclaim liberty to the captives and recovering of sight to the blind, to set at liberty those who are oppressed, to proclaim the year of the Lord's favour." (*Lk* 4:18b-19)

6 *Hail Mary...*

And he began to say to them, "Today this scripture has been fulfilled in your hearing." And all spoke well of him and marvelled at the gracious words that were coming out of his mouth. (*Lk* 4:21-22a)

7 *Hail Mary...*

And he went throughout all Galilee, teaching in their synagogues and proclaiming the gospel of the kingdom and healing every disease and every affliction among the people. (*Mt* 4:23)

8 *Hail Mary...*

So his fame spread throughout all Syria, and they brought him all the sick, those afflicted with various diseases and pains, those oppressed by demons, those having seizures, and paralytics, and he healed them. (*Mt* 4:24)

9 *Hail Mary...*

And they were all amazed, so that they questioned among themselves, saying, "What is this? A new teaching with authority! He commands even the unclean spirits, and they obey him." And at once his fame spread everywhere throughout all the surrounding region of Galilee. (*Mk* 1:27-28)

Hail Mary...

And he said to them, "Let us go on to the next towns, that I may preach there also, for that is what I came for." And he went throughout all Galilee, preaching in their synagogues and casting out demons. (*Mk* 1:38-39)

Glory be to the Father...

FOURTH LUMINOUS MYSTERY

The Transfiguration

The Transfiguration is the most radiant of the Mysteries of Light. We contemplate the glory of the Godhead shining forth from the face of Christ as the Father commands the astonished Apostles to "listen to him". We pray that as we may be called to share in his sufferings, so we may come with him to a life transfigured by the Holy Spirit and the glory of the Resurrection.

We have seen his glory, glory as of the only Son from the Father. (*Jn* 1:14)
Our Father...

Jesus took with him Peter and James and John, and led them up a high mountain by themselves. And he was transfigured before them. (*Mk* 9:2)
Hail Mary...

And as he was praying, the appearance of his face was altered (*Lk* 9:29), and his clothes became radiant, intensely white, as no one on earth could bleach them (*Mk* 9:3).
Hail Mary...

And behold, two men were talking with him, Moses and Elijah, who appeared in glory and spoke of his departure, which he was about to accomplish at Jerusalem. (*Lk* 9:31)
Hail Mary...

Now Peter and those who were with him were heavy with sleep, but when they became fully awake they saw his glory and the two men who stood with him. (*Lk* 9:32) And Peter said to Jesus, "Lord, it is good that we are here. If you wish, I will make three tents here, one for you and one for Moses and one for Elijah." (*Mt* 17:4)
Hail Mary...

As he was saying these things, a cloud came and overshadowed them, and they were afraid as they entered the cloud. (*Lk* 9:34)
Hail Mary...

And a voice came out of the cloud, saying, "This is my Son, my Chosen One; listen to him!" (*Lk* 9:35)

6 *Hail Mary…*

When the disciples heard this, they fell on their faces, and were terrified. (*Mt* 17:6)

7 *Hail Mary…*

But Jesus came and touched them, saying, "Rise, and have no fear." (*Mt* 17:7)

8 *Hail Mary…*

And suddenly, looking around, they no longer saw any one with them but Jesus only. (*Mk* 9:8)

9 *Hail Mary…*

And as they were coming down the mountain, Jesus commanded them, "Tell no one the vision, until the Son of Man is raised from the dead." (*Mt* 17:9)

10 *Hail Mary…*

So they kept the matter to themselves, questioning what this rising from the dead meant. (*Mk* 9:10)

✠ *Glory be to the Father...*

FIFTH LUMINOUS MYSTERY

The Institution of the Blessed Eucharist

The institution of the Eucharist is the last and greatest Mystery of Light, in which Christ offers us his Body and Blood as food under the appearances of bread and wine as a memorial of his sacrifice on the Cross and as the continuation of his presence among us. As we rejoice in this wonderful gift of himself to us, we pray that we may one day become sharers in the heavenly banquet to which the Mass looks forward.

Jesus said, "I am the bread of life; whoever comes to me shall not hunger, and whoever believes in me shall never thirst." (*Jn* 6:35)

Our Father...

Now before the Feast of the Passover, when Jesus knew that his hour had come to depart out of this world to the Father, having loved his own who were in the world, he loved them to the end. (*Jn* 13:1)

Hail Mary...

And he said to them, "I have earnestly desired to eat this Passover with you before I suffer." (*Lk* 22:15)

Hail Mary...

"For I tell you I shall not eat it until it is fulfilled in the kingdom of God." (*Lk* 22:16)

Hail Mary...

Now as they were eating, Jesus took bread, and after blessing it broke it and gave it to the disciples, and said, "Take, eat; this is my body." (*Mt* 26:26) "Do this in remembrance of me." (*Lk* 22:19)

Hail Mary...

And he took a cup, and when he had given thanks he said, "Take this, and divide it among yourselves." (*Lk* 22:17) And they all drank of it. (*Mk* 14:23)

Hail Mary...

"For this is my blood of the covenant, which is poured out for many for the forgiveness of sins." (*Mt* 26:28)
Hail Mary…

"For I tell you that from now on I shall not drink of the fruit of the vine until the kingdom of God comes." (*Lk* 22:18)
Hail Mary…

"I am the living bread that came down from heaven. If any one eats of this bread, he will live for ever. And the bread that I will give for the life of the world is my flesh." (*Jn* 6:51)
Hail Mary…

So Jesus said to them, "Truly, truly, I say to you, unless you eat the flesh of the Son of Man and drink his blood, you have no life in you." (*Jn* 6:53)
Hail Mary…

"Whoever feeds on my flesh and drinks my blood has eternal life, and I will raise him up at the last day. For my flesh is true food, and my blood is true drink." (*Jn* 6:54-55)
Hail Mary…

"Whoever feeds on my flesh and drinks my blood abides in me, and I in him. As the living Father sent me, and I live because of the Father, so whoever feeds on me, he also will live because of me." (*Jn* 6:56-57)
Glory be to the Father…

The Sorrowful Mysteries of the Rosary

In the Sorrowful Mysteries we encounter five different kinds of suffering endured for us by Christ, and which he asks us to be ready to share with him when he calls upon us to take up our cross each day and follow him.

FIRST SORROWFUL MYSTERY

The Agony and Prayer of Our Lord in the Garden of Gethsemane

The Agony and Prayer of Our Lord in the Garden of Gethsemane show us the terrible mental sufferings which heralded his Passion. St John Henry (Cardinal) Newman refers to "the double agony" that Christ underwent for us, meaning both the mental and bodily sufferings which together comprised his bitter Passion. We pray that his sufferings may not be in vain, but that by them we may be brought safely to heaven.

"Now is my soul troubled. And what shall I say? 'Father, save me from this hour'? But for this purpose I have come to this hour. Father, glorify your name." Then a voice came from heaven, "I have glorified it, and I will glorify it again." The crowd that stood there and heard it said that it had thundered. Others said, "An angel has spoken to him." Jesus answered, "This voice has come for your sake, not mine." (*Jn* 12:27-30)

Our Father...

Then Jesus went with them to a place called Gethsemane, and he said to his disciples, "Sit here, while I go over there and pray." (*Mt* 26:36)

Hail Mary...

And when he came to the place, he said to them, "Pray that you may not enter into temptation." (*Lk* 22:40)

Hail Mary...

And taking with him Peter and the two sons of Zebedee, he began to be sorrowful and troubled.. (*Mt* 26:37)

Hail Mary...

Then he said to them, "My soul is very sorrowful, even to death; remain here, and watch with me." (*Mt* 26:38)

Hail Mary...

And going a little farther he fell on his face and prayed, saying "My Father, if it be possible, let this cup pass from me; nevertheless, not as I will, but as you will." (*Mt* 26:39)

Hail Mary...

And there appeared to him an angel from heaven, strengthening him. And being in agony he prayed more earnestly; and his sweat became like great drops of blood falling down to the ground. (*Lk* 22:43-44)

6 *Hail Mary...*

He came to the disciples and found them sleeping. "So, could you not watch with me one hour? Watch and pray that you may not enter into temptation. The spirit indeed is willing, but the flesh is weak." (*Mt* 26:40-41)

7 *Hail Mary...*

Again, for the second time, he went away and prayed, "My Father, if this cannot pass unless I drink it, your will be done!" (*Mt* 26:42)

8 *Hail Mary...*

And when he rose from prayer, he came to the disciples and found them sleeping for sorrow, and he said to them "Why are you sleeping? Rise and pray that you might not enter into temptation." (*Lk* 22:45-46)

9 *Hail Mary...*

So, leaving them again, he went away and prayed for the third time, saying the same words again. (*Mt* 26:44)

10 *Hail Mary...*

Then he came to the disciples and said, "Sleep and take your rest later on. See, the hour is at hand, and the Son of Man is betrayed into the hands of sinners. Rise, let us be going; see, my betrayer is at hand." (*Mt* 26:45-46)

✠ *Glory be to the Father...*

SECOND SORROWFUL MYSTERY

Our Lord is Scourged at the Pillar

In the Scourging, we see the pain and sorrow of the torture and bodily suffering and disfigurement of Jesus "by whose wounds we are healed" (*1 P* 2:24). We pray for the grace to endure whatever painful sufferings God may ask us to bear for love of him, in order to fulfil "in our flesh…what is lacking in Christ's afflictions for the sake of his body, that is, the church" (*Col* 1:24).

Pilate said to them, "Then what shall I do with Jesus who is called Christ?" They all said, "Let him be crucified!" And he said, "Why? What evil has he done?" But they shouted all the more, "Let him be crucified!" (*Mt* 27:22-23)

Our Father...

So when Pilate saw that he was gaining nothing, but rather that a riot was beginning, he took water and washed his hands before the crowd, saying, "I am innocent of this man's blood; see to it yourselves." (*Mt* 27:24)

Hail Mary...

And all the people, answered, "His blood be on us and on our children!" Then he released for them Barabbas, and having scourged Jesus, delivered him to be crucified. (*Mt* 27:25-26)

Hail Mary...

Behold, my servant shall act wisely; he shall be high and lifted up, and shall be exalted. (*Is* 52:13)

Hail Mary...

His appearance was so marred, beyond human semblance, and his form beyond that of the children of mankind – so shall he startle[6] many nations. Kings shall shut their mouths because of him. (Is 52:14-15a)

Hail Mary...

---

6 The Hebrew word for 'startle' is also translated as 'sprinkle'.

For that which has not been told them they see, and that which they have not heard they understand. Who has believed what he has heard from us? And to whom has the arm of the Lord been revealed?" (*Is* 52:15b-53:1)

Hail Mary...

For he grew up before him like a young plant, and like a root out of dry ground; he had no form or majesty that we should look at him, and no beauty that we should desire him. (*Is* 53:2)

Hail Mary...

He was despised and rejected by men, a man of sorrows and acquainted with grief; as one from whom men hide their faces; he was despised, and we esteemed him not. (*Is* 53:3)

Hail Mary...

Surely he has borne our griefs and carried our sorrows; yet we esteemed him stricken, smitten by God and afflicted. (*Is* 53:4)

Hail Mary...

But he was pierced for our transgressions; he was crushed for our iniquities; upon him was the chastisement that brought us peace, and with his wounds we are healed. (*Is* 53:5)

Hail Mary...

5
6
7
8
9

All we like sheep have gone astray; we have turned – every one – to his own way; and the Lord has laid on him the iniquity of us all. (*Is* 53:6)

10 *Hail Mary...*

He was oppressed, and he was afflicted, yet he opened not his mouth; like a lamb that is led to the slaughter, and like a sheep that before its shearers is silent, so he opened not his mouth. (*Is* 53:7)

✠ *Glory be to the Father...*

THIRD SORROWFUL MYSTERY

Our Lord is Crowned with Thorns

In the Crowning with Thorns we see exemplified Christ the King's suffering of humiliation and mockery. We contemplate our Lord's humble submission to the vicious cruelty of wicked men and pray that we may be prepared to endure the ridicule of others rather than deny our Lord.

The Lord has opened my ear, and I was not rebellious; I turned not backwards. I gave my back to those who strike, and my cheeks to those who pull out the beard; I hid not my face from disgrace and spitting. (*Is* 50:5-6)

Our Father...

So Pilate entered his headquarters again and called Jesus and said to him, "Are you the king of the Jews?" Jesus answered, "Do you say this of your own accord, or did others say it to you about me?" (*Jn* 18:33-34)

Hail Mary...

Pilate answered, "Am I a Jew? Your own nation and the chief priests have delivered you over to me. What have you done?" (*Jn* 18:35)

Hail Mary...

Jesus answered, "My kingdom is not of this world. If my kingdom were of this world, my servants would have been fighting, that I might not be delivered over to the Jews. But my kingdom is not from the world." (*Jn* 18:36)

Hail Mary...

Then Pilate said to him, "So you are a king?" Jesus answered, "You say that I am a king." (*Jn* 18:37a)

Hail Mary...

"For this purpose I was born and for this purpose I came into the world – to bear witness to the truth. Everyone who is of the truth listens to my voice." (*Jn* 18:37b)

Hail Mary...

Then the soldiers of the governor took Jesus into the governor's headquarters, and they gathered the whole battalion before him. And they stripped him and put a scarlet robe on him, and twisting together a crown of thorns, they put it on his head and put a reed in his right hand. (*Mt* 27:27-29a)

Hail Mary...

And kneeling before him, they mocked him, saying, "Hail, king of the Jews!" And they spat on him and took the reed and struck him on the head. (*Mt* 27:29b-30)

Hail Mary...

Pilate went out again and said to them, "See, I am bringing him out to you that you may know that I find no guilt in him". (*Jn* 19:4)

Hail Mary...

So Jesus came out, wearing the crown of thorns and the purple robe. Pilate said to them, "Behold the man!" (*Jn* 19:5)

Hail Mary...

Pilate said to the Jews, "Behold your King!" They cried out, "Away with him, away with him, crucify him!" Pilate said to them, "Shall I crucify your King?" (*Jn* 19:14b-15a)

Hail Mary...

The chief priests answered, "We have no king but Caesar." So he delivered him over to them to be crucified. (*Jn* 19:15b-16)

Glory be to the Father...

FOURTH SORROWFUL MYSTERY

Our Lord Carries his Cross to Calvary

In the carrying of the Cross we contemplate our Lord's bodily exhaustion. When, like Simon of Cyrene, we carry our Lord's Cross with him, our work and even our exhaustion can be turned to a good purpose and sanctified. We pray that our labours may be a co-operation with our Lord in the work of our redemption.

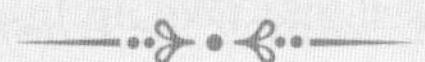

The godless say to themselves, "Let us lie in wait for the righteous man...let us test what will happen at the end of his life; for if the righteous man is God's son, he will help him and will deliver him from the hands of his adversaries. Let us test him with insult and torture...and make trial of his forbearance. Let us condemn him to a shameful death for, according to what he says, he will be protected." (*Ws* 2:12, 17-20)

Our Father...

Jesus said to his disciples, "The Son of Man must suffer many things and be rejected by the elders and chief priests and scribes, and be killed, and on the third day be raised." (*Lk* 9:22)

Hail Mary...

And he said to all, "If anyone would come after me, let him deny himself and take up his cross daily and follow me." (*Lk* 9:23)

Hail Mary...

"For whoever would save his life will lose it, but whoever loses his life for my sake will save it." (*Lk* 9:24)

Hail Mary...

So Pilate decided that their demand should be granted. He released the man who had been imprisoned for insurrection and murder, for whom they asked, but he delivered Jesus over to their will. (*Lk* 23:24-25)

Hail Mary...

So they took Jesus, and he went out, bearing his own cross, to the place called The Place of a Skull which in Aramaic is called Golgotha. *(Jn 19:17)*

5 *Hail Mary...*

And as they led him away, they seized one Simon of Cyrene, who was coming in from the country, and laid on him the cross, to carry it behind Jesus. (*Lk* 23:26)

6 *Hail Mary...*

And there followed him a great multitude of the people and of women who were mourning and lamenting for him. (*Lk* 23:27)

7 *Hail Mary...*

But turning to them Jesus said, "Daughters of Jerusalem, do not weep for me, but weep for yourselves and for your children." (*Lk* 23:28)

8 *Hail Mary...*

"For behold, the days are coming when they will say, 'Blessed are the barren and the wombs that never bore and the breasts that never nursed!' Then they will begin to say to the mountains, 'Fall on us' and to the hills, 'Cover us.' For if they do these things when the wood is green, what will happen when it is dry?" (*Lk* 23:29-31)

9 *Hail Mary...*

And when they came to a place called Golgotha (which means Place of a Skull), they offered him wine to drink, mixed with gall, but when he tasted it, he would not drink it. (*Mt* 27:33-34)

Hail Mary...

And when they came to the place that is called The Skull, there they crucified him, and the criminals, one on his right and one on his left. And Jesus said, "Father, forgive them, for they know not what they do." (*Lk* 23:33-34a)

Glory be to the Father...

FIFTH SORROWFUL MYSTERY

The Crucifixion and Death of Our Lord

The Death of Our Lord on the Cross signifies to us that event which, despite all differences in our lives and circumstances, will nevertheless befall us all equally: the death of the body. We pray for the grace to accept whatever death God will send us, accompanied by whatever pain and dereliction he chooses as the means of uniting ourselves in that moment with our crucified Saviour.

Jesus said to Nicodemus, "As Moses lifted up the serpent in the wilderness, so must the Son of Man be lifted up, that whoever believes in him may have eternal life." (*Jn* 3:14) "Now is the judgement of this world; now will the ruler of this world be cast out. And I, when I am lifted up from the earth, will draw all people to myself." (*Jn* 12:31-32)

Our Father...

And when they had crucified him, they divided his garments among them by casting lots. Then they sat down and kept watch over him there. (*Mt* 27:35-36)

Hail Mary...

And over his head they put the charge against him, which read: "This is Jesus, the King of the Jews". (*Mt* 27:37)

Hail Mary...

And those who passed by derided him, wagging their heads and saying, "Aha! You who would destroy the temple and rebuild it in three days, save yourself, and come down from the cross!" (*Mk* 15:29-30)

Hail Mary...

So also the chief priests with the scribes mocked him to one another, saying, "He saved others; he cannot save himself. Let the Christ, the King of Israel, come down now from the cross that we may see and believe." (*Mk* 15: 31-32a)

Hail Mary...

One of the criminals who were hanged railed at him, saying, “Are you not the Christ? Save yourself and us!”. But the other rebuked him, saying, “Do you not fear God, since you are under the same sentence of condemnation? And we indeed justly, for we are receiving the due reward of our deeds; but this man has done nothing wrong.” (*Lk* 23:39-41)

Hail Mary...

And he said, “Jesus, remember me when you come into your kingdom.” And he said to him, “Truly, I say to you, today you will be with me in paradise.” (*Lk* 23:42-43)

Hail Mary...

When Jesus saw his mother and the disciple whom he loved standing nearby, he said to his mother, “Woman, behold, your son!” Then he said to the disciple, “Behold, your mother!” (*Jn* 19:26-27a)

Hail Mary...

And when the sixth hour had come, there was darkness over the whole land until the ninth hour. And at the ninth hour Jesus cried with a loud voice, “Eloi, Eloi, lema sabachthani?” which means “My God, My God, why have you forsaken me?” (*Mk* 15:33-34)

Hail Mary...

After this, Jesus, knowing that all was now finished, said (to fulfil the Scripture), “I thirst”. A jar full of sour wine stood there, so they put a sponge full of the sour wine on a hyssop branch and held it to his mouth.

When Jesus had received the sour wine, he said, "It is finished". (*Jn* 19:28-30a)
Hail Mary...

Then Jesus, calling out with a loud voice, said, "Father, into your hands I commit my spirit!" And having said this he breathed his last. (*Lk* 23:46)
Hail Mary...

And the curtain of the temple was torn in two, from top to bottom. And when the centurion, who stood facing him, saw that in this way he breathed his last, he said, "Truly, this man was the Son of God!" (*Mk* 15:38-39)
Glory be to the Father...

The Glorious Mysteries of the Rosary

In the Glorious Mysteries we contemplate five elements that characterise and contribute to the eternal glory of heaven as the goal and true purpose of our existence in God's plan.

FIRST GLORIOUS MYSTERY

The Resurrection of Our Lord from the Dead on Easter Day

In the Resurrection we contemplate the reality of life triumphant over death; that life which endures and even swallows up death which previously seemed to have annihilated life itself. We recollect with joy and confidence, that Christ's resurrection is the cause of our own future rising from the grave. We pray that we may always be filled with the hope of glory that Christ's resurrection brings.

The Lord's right hand has triumphed; his right hand raised me up. I shall not die, I shall live and recount his deeds. (*Ps* 117 (*Hebr Ps* 118):16-17)

Our Father...

Now after the Sabbath, towards the dawn of the first day of the week, Mary Magdalene and the other Mary went to see the tomb. And behold, there was a great earthquake, for an angel of the Lord descended from heaven and came and rolled back the stone and sat on it. His appearance was like lightning, and his clothing white as snow. (*Mt* 28:1-3)

Hail Mary...

And for fear of him the guards trembled and became like dead men. But the angel said to the women, "Do not be afraid, for I know you seek Jesus who was crucified. He is not here, for he has risen, as he said." (*Mt* 28:4-6)

Hail Mary...

Mary Magdalene ran and went to Simon Peter and the other disciple, the one whom Jesus loved, and said to them, "They have taken the Lord out of the tomb, and we do not know where they have laid him." (*Jn* 20:2)

Hail Mary...

So Peter went out with the other disciple, and they were going towards the tomb. Both of them were running together, but the other disciple outran Peter and reached the tomb first. And stooping to look in, he saw the linen cloths lying there, but he did not go in. (*Jn* 20:3-5)

Hail Mary...

Then Simon Peter came, following him, and went into the tomb. He saw the linen cloths lying there, and the face cloth, which had been on Jesus's head, not lying with the linen cloths but folded up in a place by itself. (*Jn* 20:6-7)

Hail Mary...

Then the other disciple, who had reached the tomb first, also went in, and he saw and believed; for as yet they did not understand the Scripture, that he must rise from the dead. (*Jn* 20:8-9)

Hail Mary...

And behold, Jesus met them and said, "Greetings!" And they came up and took hold of his feet and worshipped him. (*Mt* 28:9)

Hail Mary...

On the evening of that day, the first day of the week, the doors being locked where the disciples were, for fear of the Jews, Jesus came and stood among them and said to them, "Peace be with you." When he had said this, he showed them his hands and his side. (*Jn* 20:19-20a)

Hail Mary...

Then the disciples were glad when they saw the Lord. Jesus said to them again, "Peace be with you. As the Father has sent me, even so I am sending you." (*Jn* 20:20b-21)

Hail Mary...

And when he had said this, he breathed on them and said to them, "Receive the Holy Spirit. If you forgive the sins of any, they are forgiven them." (*Jn* 20:22-23a)

Hail Mary...

Now Thomas, one of the twelve, called the Twin, was not with them when Jesus came....Eight days later, his disciples were inside again, and Thomas was with them. Although the doors were locked, Jesus came and stood among them and said, "Peace be with you." Then he said to Thomas, "Put your finger here, and see my hands; And put out your hand, and place it in my side. Do not disbelieve, but believe." Thomas answered him, "My Lord and my God!" (*Jn* 20:24, 26-28)

Glory be to the Father...

SECOND GLORIOUS MYSTERY

The Ascension of Our Lord to the Right Hand of the Father in Heaven

In the Ascension we contemplate Christ's entry as both man and God into the glorious and everlasting life of heaven. We pray that we may be made fit for the vision of God and may be prepared to share in eternal glory by the purification and freeing of our faculties from all that binds them to the earth and to this life.

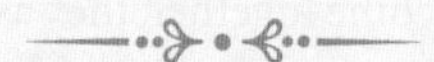

All peoples, clap your hands, cry to God with shouts of joy! For the Lord, the Most High, we must fear, great king over all the earth. God goes up with shouts of joy; the Lord goes up with trumpet blast. (*Ps* 46 (*Hebr Ps* 47): 1-2, 6)

Our Father...

Jesus presented himself alive to his disciples after his suffering by many proofs, appearing to them during forty days and speaking about the kingdom of God. (*Ac* 1:3)

Hail Mary...

Now the eleven disciples went to Galilee, to the mountain to which Jesus had directed them. And when they saw him worshipped him, but some doubted. (*Mt* 28:16-17)

Hail Mary...

So when they had come together, they asked him, "Lord, will you at this time restore the kingdom to Israel?" (*Ac* 1:6)

Hail Mary...

He said to them, "It is not for you to know times or seasons that the Father has fixed by his own authority. But you will receive power when the Holy Spirit has come upon you, and you will be my witnesses in Jerusalem and in all Judaea and Samaria, and to the ends of the earth." (*Ac* 1:7-8)

Hail Mary...

And Jesus came and said to them, "All authority in heaven and on earth has been given to me. Go therefore and make disciples of all nations, baptising them in the name of the Father and of the Son and of the Holy Spirit, teaching them to observe all that I have commanded you." (*Mt* 28:18-20a)

5 *Hail Mary...*

Jesus said to them, "Go into all the world and proclaim the gospel to the whole creation. Whoever believes and is baptised will be saved, but whoever does not believe will be condemned." (*Mk* 16:15-16)

6 *Hail Mary...*

"And these signs will accompany those who believe: in my name they will cast out demons; they will speak in new tongues; they will pick up serpents with their hands; and if they drink any deadly poison, it will not hurt them; they will lay their hands on the sick, and they will recover." (*Mk* 16:17-18)

7 *Hail Mary...*

"And behold, I am sending the promise of my Father upon you. But stay in the city until you are clothed with power from on high." (*Lk* 24:49)

8 *Hail Mary...*

And he led them out as far as Bethany, and lifting up his hands he blessed them. (*Lk* 24:50)

9 *Hail Mary...*

While he blessed them, he parted from them and was carried up into heaven. And they worshipped him and returned to Jerusalem with great joy. (*Lk* 24:51-52)

Hail Mary...

So then the Lord Jesus, after he had spoken to them, was taken up into heaven and sat down at the right hand of God. (*Mk* 16:19)

Glory be to the Father...

THIRD GLORIOUS MYSTERY

The Descent of the Holy Spirit on the Apostles and Our Lady on the Day of Pentecost

The Holy Spirit descends from the Father and the Son in order to implant in us the seeds of union with God and to foster their growth. By the anointing of the Spirit, we are enabled to arrive at the holiness which will enable us to ascend to heaven.We pray that through the Sacraments and the life of grace we may be drawn on towards our final sharing in the fulness of the life of the Blessed Trinity.

"And it shall come to pass afterwards, that I will pour out my Spirit on all flesh; your sons and your daughters shall prophesy, your old men shall dream dreams, and your young men shall see visions. Even on the male and female servants in those days I will pour out my Spirit.. (*Jl* 2:28-29 (*Hebr Jl* 3:1-2))

Our Father...

On the last day of the feast, the great day, Jesus stood up and cried out: "If anyone thirsts, let him come to me and drink. Whoever believes in me, as the Scripture has said, 'Out of his heart will flow rivers of living water.'" (*Jn* 7:37-38)

Hail Mary...

Now this he said about the Spirit, whom those who believed in him were to receive, for as yet the Spirit had not been given, because Jesus was not yet glorified. (*Jn* 7:39)

Hail Mary...

At the Last Supper Jesus said to his disciples, "I still have many things to say to you, but you cannot bear them now. When the Spirit of truth comes, he will guide you into all the truth." (*Jn* 16:12-13a)

Hail Mary...

Then the Apostles returned to Jerusalem...and when they had entered, they went up to the upper room, where they were staying...All these with one accord were devoting themselves to prayer, together with the women and Mary the mother of Jesus, and his brothers. (*Ac* 1:12a, 13a, 14)

4 *Hail Mary...*

When the day of Pentecost arrived, they were all together in one place. And suddenly there came from heaven a sound like a mighty rushing wind, and it filled the entire house where they were sitting. (*Ac* 2:1-2)

5 *Hail Mary...*

And divided tongues as of fire appeared to them and rested on each one of them. (*Ac* 2:3)

6 *Hail Mary...*

And they were all filled with the Holy Spirit and began to speak in other tongues as the Spirit gave them utterance. (*Ac* 2:4)

7 *Hail Mary...*

Now there were dwelling in Jerusalem Jews, devout men from every nation under heaven. And at this sound the multitude came together, and they were bewildered, because each one was hearing them speak in his own language. (*Ac* 2:5-6)

8 *Hail Mary...*

And they were amazed and astonished, saying "Are not all these who are speaking Galilaeans? And how is it that we hear, each of us in his own native language?... We hear them telling in our own tongues the mighty works of God." (*Ac* 2:7-8, 11b)

9 *Hail Mary...*

While Peter was still saying these things, the Holy Spirit fell on all who heard the word. And the believers from among the circumcised who had come with Peter were amazed, because the gift of the Holy Spirit was poured out even on the Gentiles. (*Ac* 10:44-45)

Hail Mary...

Then Peter declared, "Can anyone withhold water for baptising these people, who have received the Holy Spirit just as we have?" (*Ac* 10:46-47)

Glory be to the Father...

FOURTH GLORIOUS MYSTERY

The Assumption of Our Blessed Lady, Body and Soul, to the Glory of Heaven

In the Assumption of Our Lady we see the first fruits of the Resurrection. She is the first of redeemed humanity. Hence, in Mary we are promised the raising of our bodily lives to a newly glorified state. We pray to be reunited with all those whom we have known and loved in this life and to see the restoration and fulfilment of all that human love and friendship has ever given us.

The daughters of kings are among your loved ones. On your right stands the queen in gold of Ophir. Listen, O daughter, give ear to my words: forget your own people and your father's house. (*Ps* 44 (*Hebr Ps* 45):10-11)

Our Father...

I will greatly rejoice in the Lord; my soul shall exult in my God (*Is* 61:10a)

Hail Mary...

For he has clothed me with the garments of salvation; he has covered me with the robe of righteousness, as a bridegroom decks himself like a priest with a beautiful headdress, and as a bride adorns herself with her jewels. (*Is* 61:10b)

Hail Mary...

For as the earth brings forth its sprouts, and as a garden causes what is sown in it to sprout up, so the Lord God will cause righteousness and praise to sprout up before all the nations. (*Is* 61:11)

Hail Mary...

Then God's temple in heaven was opened, and the ark of his covenant was seen within his temple. (*Rv* 11:19a)

Hail Mary...

And a great sign appeared in heaven: a woman clothed with the sun, with the moon under her feet, and on her head a crown of twelve stars. (*Rv* 12:1)

Hail Mary...

She gave birth to a male child, one who is to rule all the nations with a rod of iron. (*Rv* 12:5a)

6 *Hail Mary...*

But her child was caught up to God and to his throne, and the woman fled into the wilderness, where she has a place prepared by God. (*Rv* 12:5b-6)

7 *Hail Mary...*

My beloved speaks and says to me, "Arise, my love, my beautiful one, and come away, for behold, the winter is past; the rain is over and gone." (*Sg* 2:10-11)

8 *Hail Mary...*

"Arise, my love, my beautiful one, and come away. O my dove, in the clefts of the rock, in the crannies of the cliff, let me see your face, let me hear your voice, for your voice is sweet, and your face is lovely." (*Sg* 2:13b-14)

9 *Hail Mary...*

"You are altogether beautiful, my love; there is no flaw in you." (*Sg* 4:7)

10 *Hail Mary...*

"Who is this who looks down like the dawn, beautiful as the moon, bright as the sun, awesome as an army with banners?" (*Sg* 6:10)

✠ *Glory be to the Father...*

FIFTH GLORIOUS MYSTERY

The Coronation of Our Blessed Lady, as Queen of Heaven and the Glory of all the Saints

The Coronation of Our Lady and the glory of all the saints tells us of the reward of all our striving. St Paul prepares us to enter into 'what no eye has seen, nor ear heard, nor the heart of man imagined, what God has prepared for those who love him' (*1 Co* 2:9). We pray that all those things which we have been unable to understand but have offered to God out of love for him and trusting in his providence, will be revealed to us in their fulness as our crown of glory in heaven.

For Zion's sake I will not keep silent, and for Jerusalem's sake I will not be quiet, until her righteousness goes forth as brightness, and her salvation as a burning torch. (*Is* 62:1)

Our Father...

You shall be a crown of beauty in the hand of the Lord, and a royal diadem in the hand of your God. (*Is* 62:3)

Hail Mary...

For as a young man marries a young woman, so shall your sons marry you, and as the bridegroom rejoices over the bride, so shall your God rejoice over you. (*Is* 62:5)

Hail Mary...

Beloved, we are God's children now, and what we will be has not yet appeared; but we know that when he appears we shall be like him, because we shall see him as he is. (*1 Jn* 3:2)

Hail Mary...

Then I, John, saw a new heaven and a new earth, for the first heaven and the first earth had passed away, and the sea was no more. (*Rv* 21:1)

Hail Mary...

And I saw the holy city, new Jerusalem, coming down out of heaven from God, prepared as a bride adorned for her husband. (*Rv* 21:2)

Hail Mary...

And I heard a loud voice from the throne saying, "Behold, the dwelling place of God is with man." (*Rv* 21:3a)

Hail Mary...

He will dwell with them, and they will be his people, and God himself will be with them as their God. (*Rv* 21:3b)

Hail Mary...

He will wipe away every tear from their eyes; and death shall be no more, neither shall there be mourning, nor crying, nor pain any more, for the former things have passed away. (*Rv* 21:4)

Hail Mary...

And he who was seated on the throne said, "Behold, I am making all things new." (*Rv* 21:5a)

Hail Mary...

"Behold, I am coming soon, bringing my recompense with me, to repay each one for what he has done." (*Rv* 22:12)

Hail Mary...

"I am the Alpha and the Omega, the first and the last, the beginning and the end." (*Rv* 22:13)

Glory be to the Father...

Image Credits

Page 4: *Madonna and Child* by Borgognone. Purchased with the support of the Vereniging Rembrandt, Rijksmuseum, Amsterdam.

Page 18: *The Nativity with Donors and Saints Jerome and Leonard* by Gerard David. The Jules Bache Collection, 1949, The Metropolitan Museum of Art.

Page 38: *The Baptism of Christ*, Four Panels from the San Lazaro Altarpiece by Juan de Flandes. Samuel H. Kress Collection, National Gallery of Art, Washington.

Page 56: *The Crucifixion* by Gerard David. Rogers Fund, 1909. The Metropolitan Museum of Art.

Page 76: *The Resurrection*, by circle of Master of the Amsterdam Death of the Virgin. Rijksmuseum, Amsterdam.